JAPAN'S
WAR IN CHINA

By

HU SHIH

Chinese Ambassador
to the United States of America

Japan's War In China

Hu Shih

JAPAN'S WAR IN CHINA

Resumé of an Address by His Excellency Dr. Hu Shih, Chinese Ambassador to the United States of America. New York, December 4, 1938.

If I were asked to sum up in one sentence the present conditions in my country, I would not hesitate to say that China is literally bleeding to death.

We have been fighting for more than sixteen months against an aggressor which is one of the three greatest naval powers, and one of the four or five greatest military powers of the world. We have suffered one million casualties, including the killed and the wounded. We have vast territories being occupied by the invading armies. We have lost all the important cities on the coast and along the Yangtse River: Peiping, Tientsin, Tsingtao, Tsinan, Shanghai, Hangchow, Nanking, Wuhu, Kiukiang, Amoy, Canton and the Wu-Han cities. Practically all the cities that are generally known to the outside world as centers of commerce and industry, of education and modern culture, of transportation and communication, are now either devastated or occupied by the invaders. Of the 111 universities and colleges, more than two-thirds have been either destroyed, occupied, or disabled; and the very few that are still functioning in the interior are working without equipment and under constant dangers of air raids. And, in addition to the vast number of casualties in the fighting forces, there are now 60 million civilian sufferers who have been driven from their destroyed homes, farms, shops and villages, and who are fleeing the invader and are roving the country without shelter, without medical aid, and in most cases without the barest means of subsistence. And there are every day hundreds of innocent non-combatants being murdered and slaughtered by the bombers of the Imperial Army of Japan.

And, most serious of all, with the loss of Canton in October, China is now entirely cut off from all access to the sea,—that is, from all access to fresh supplies of arms and munitions from abroad. We have to rely upon three back doors for future war supplies from abroad, namely, the overland route to Soviet Russia, the route through French Indo-China, and the route through British Burma. All these three routes are very difficult and not always dependable. After repeated threats from Japan, the French are reported to have now closed the Indo-China Railway to Chinese munitions. The overland motor road to Soviet Russia is open, but it is 3,000 miles from the Russian border to the present capital at Chungking, a distance longer than that from San Francisco to New York. No heavy pieces of munitions can be transported over such a long road with very few service stations. The Burma route is not yet quite ready for use. So for the present we are actually completely cut off from the sea and from our sinews of war. This also means that we are faced with tremendous difficulties in sending out our exports with which to secure our foreign exchange.

This is our present situation. Have I overstated the case in saying that China is literally bleeding to death?

3

It was natural that, after the fall of Canton and Hankow, there was a brief period of doubt, hesitation and even despair on the part of many of our people and of our leaders. As I have repeatedly pointed out to my American friends, there is a limit to the ability of human flesh and blood to fight against much superior mechanical and metal equipment; and there is always the danger of collapse through sheer exhaustion. It was quite natural, therefore, that my people should have had this period of doubt and indecision during which, as the press reported, there were talks of peace,—that is, there were serious thoughts of giving up the fight. In fact, our enemy, too, made it quite clear that they wanted peace.

. But this period of hesitation was also a period of great decisions. It did not take very long for our leaders to come to the conclusion that it was impossible for China to have peace at the present moment simply because there was not the slightest chance for a peace that would be reasonably acceptable to my people. After serious considerations of all difficulties and potentialities, our leaders have definitely decided to continue our policy of resisting the invader and to fight on.

In announcing this new determination to the nation and to the world at large, Generalissimo Chiang Kai-shek laid special stress on these points: that China will continue her policy of prolonged nation-wide resistance; that as the war has become really "nation-wide" and the enemy is drawn into the interior, both time and geography are on our side; that our war of resistance during the past 16 months has succeeded in retarding the westward advance of the enemy, thus enabling ourselves to develop communications and transportations in the vast hinterland and remove some industries thither; that we can only hope to win final victory through the greatest hardship and sacrifice; and that this war of resistance must be understood as a "revolutionary warfare" similar to the wars of American Independence, French and Russian Revolution and Turkish Emancipation, and in such revolutionary warfare the spirit of the people will ultimately win out.

This is the solemn declaration of China's new determination.

*　　*　　*　　*

What will the world think of this new decision of my people to fight on against tremendous and apparently unsurmountable difficulties? Will it regard this determination as sheer folly built upon no better foundation than the logic of wishful thinking?

Whatever the world may think of us, I can assure you that a nation that has sacrificed a million men and is prepared to make even greater sacrifices in fighting for its national existence cannot be accused of basing its hopes and aspirations upon mere wishful thinking. We are making a deliberate decision on the basis of the sixteen months' terrible but very instructive experience of the war. We have learned during these terrible months that our soldiers and officers are capable of heroic bravery and supreme sacrifices, that our

4

people are bearing their losses and devastations without complaining against their Government, and that the sense of national unity and solidarity throughout the country including the parts temporarily under the military occupation of the enemy is beyond question. And we have also learned that our enemy is actually feeling the burden of the prolonged war; that Japan's finances are nearing the breaking point; that she is employing her full armed strength in fighting a nation which she had never seriously considered as capable of putting up a fight; that she is terribly worried by the vast expenditure of her store of war munitions intended for greater wars against more formidable foes; and that it is not impossible for us to wear out our enemy if we can only fight on long enough.

* * * *

Moreover, it seems to me as an amateur historian that there is much truth in the statement that our war of resistance is a kind of "revolutionary warfare" which can best be understood in the light of the history of the revolutionary wars of America, France, Russia and Turkey. Surely an American audience can appreciate this historical analogy. Not very long ago, an American friend wrote me these words: "China is now at Valley Forge; but I hope she will soon be at Yorktown." These words were written before I read General Chiang Kai-shek's message referred to above. It may not be entirely out of place for me to develop this historical analogy a little further.

John Fiske, one of your most scientific historians, said: "The dreadful sufferings of Washington's army at Valley Forge have called forth the pity and the admiration of historians. As the poor soldiers marched on the 17th of December (1777) to their winter quarters, their route could be traced on the snow by the blood that oozed from bare, frost-bitten feet. . . . On the 23rd, Washington informed Congress that he had in camp 2,898 men 'unfit for duty, because they are barefoot, and otherwise naked.' Cold and hunger daily added many to the sick-list; and in the crowded hospitals, . . . men sometimes died for want of straw to put between themselves and the frozen ground on which they lay. So great was the distress that there were times when, in case of an attack by the enemy, scarcely two thousand men could have been got under arms." (Fiske, *The American Revolution*, II, pp. 28-29.) That was Valley Forge in the winter of 1777.

Shortly after that, the English Government under George III and Lord North offered peace by unconditionally repealing all the laws which had led to the revolt of the American Colonies. It was declared that Parliament would renounce forever the right to raise a revenue in America. And commissioners were sent to America to deal with Congress, armed with full powers to negotiate a peace.

That was an offer of an honorable peace. Had the Fathers of this Republic accepted it, it could have avoided four more years of bloodshed and sacrifice, but there would have been no Independence and no United States of America.

5

The founders of the American Republic rejected the peace of 1778 and fought on for four years longer and won the final victory at Yorktown in October, 1781.

We must remember that those intervening years were often almost as difficult and perilous as the dreary winter at Valley Forge. There were military reverses and losses of territory, and there were internal troubles and even high teason. There was nó continental government; after three years' discussion, the Articles of Confederation had not yet been adopted. The Continental Congress had rapidly declined in reputation and authority. Congress had no power to tax the States; it could only go on printing more and more "greenbacks" to finance the war. This paper money soon depreciated until, Washington said, "it took a wagon-load of money to buy a wagon-load of provisions." "Early in 1780 the value of the dollar had fallen to two cents, and by the end of the year it took ten paper dollars to make a cent. . . . The money soon ceased to circulate, debts could not be collected, and there was a general prostration of credit. . . . A barber in Philadelphia papered his shop with bills." "Under these circumstances, it became almost impossible to feed and clothe the army. . . . When four months' pay of a private soldier would not buy a single bushel of wheat for his family, and when he could not collect even this pittance, while most of the time he went bare-foot and half-famished, it was not strange that he should sometimes feel mutinous." (Fiske, *op. cit.* II, pp. 196-200.)

Such were the conditions in 1780. Yet Washington and his colleagues did not give up the fight. A year later, the final victory came at Yorktown which ended the military phase of the War of American Independence.

I have gone into some details in describing the hardships and the difficulties of the War of 1776-1781, not only to show that the conditions of the Continental Army of Washington were not much better off than those of the National Army of China in the present war, but also to illustrate what General Chiang Kai-shek means by characterizing our war of resistance as "revolutionary warfare in which the spirit of the people will ultimately win out." All revolutionary wars were fought by poorly equipped but idealistically inspired peoples against the well-equipped regular armies of an oppressor or aggressor. In the end, final victory almost invariably came to those whose idealism and heroism could overcome the greatest hardship and sacrifice.

If this is still wishful thinking, it is a type of wishful thinking so ininspiring and so enticing that millions of my people are determined to test it out with their blood and their lives.

*   *   *   *

Before concluding, I like to make another observation,—again based on historical analogy. I like to ask a question: How did the fathers of this Republic ever get out of Valley Forge and march on to the final victory of Yorktown?

6

All historians agree that two factors were responsible. The first was that the Revolutionary Army fought on in spite of almost unsurmountable difficulties. But there was another and equally important factor, namely, that the cause of the American Revolution was greatly aided by the international situation of the time. The England of George III was disliked and hated by the great powers of Europe, whose sympathies were naturally on the side of the American colonies. The Continental Congress sent a diplimatic mission to Europe, directed primarily to the French Court of Louis XVI. Among the members of the mission was Benjamin Franklin who later became the first American Minister to France, and who concluded a commercial treaty and a treaty of alliance with France and secured from France not only loans and subsidies totalling 45,000,000 *livres*, but also important military assistance in the form of a large and well-equipped expeditionary force. Even the most ardent advocate of American isolationism, Professor Samuel Flagg Bemis, tells us that "the combination of French armies and fleets in America with General Washington's forces brought about the final fortunate victory of Yorktown. The French alliance was decisive for the cause of American independence. No American should forget that." (Bemis, *A Diplomatic History of the United States,* p. 31.)

But it was not the direct assistance from France that alone was decisive for the American cause. The whole international situation at that time was directly and indirectly advantageous to the American Revolution. France and England were in an undeclared war as early as 1778. Spain declared war on England in 1779. In 1780, Empress Catherine of Russia proclaimed the principle of the freedom of the seas and the right of neutrals, a principle which was immediately accepted by all the enemies of England. In 1780, too, Holland was at war with England. But the year before the British surrender at Yorktown, England was practically at war with the whole European world and her colonial possessions everywhere were seriously menaced by France and Spain. It was this adverse international situation which made it impossible for England to reinforce her armies fighting in America and to deal any effective blow to the relatively small forces of Washington.

The moral of this historical analogy is quite clear. The final victory of China in her war of resistance to the aggressor, too, must depend upon two things: first, she must fight on, and she has no choice but to fight on; second, in her prolonged war, the time may come when the international situation may turn in her favor and against her enemy. She does not expect any other nation, however friendly and sympathetic, to take up arms and fight on her side. But she does expect, and she has a right to expect, that the sense of justice and the feeling of common humanity may yet be strong enough to move the men and women of the democratic and peace-loving countries to put a stop to the inhuman traffic of supplying weapons of war and essential raw materials for the manufacturing of weapons of war to a nation which was unanimously condemned by over 50 nations as the violator of solemnly pledged treaties and as the breaker of world peace, and which I do not hesitate to name as Public Enemy Number One among the family of nations.

7

Partial List of Publications

China Speaks on the Conflict Between China and Japan, by Chih Meng. The Macmillan Company, New York, 1932.

Memoranda Presented to the Lytton Commission, by V. K. Wellington Koo, Assessor. Three volumes. 1932.

The Broader Issues of the Sino-Japanese Question, by Sao-Ke Alfred Sze, Chinese Minister to the United States. 1932.

Some Questions Answered, by Sao-Ke Alfred Sze, Chinese Minister to the United States. 1933.

Reconstruction in China, by Sao-Ke Alfred Sze, Chinese Minister to the United States. 1934.

The Far Eastern Problem and World Peace, by The Rt. Hon. The Earl of Lytton. 1935.

American Press Opinion on the Sino-Japanese Conflict, by M. Hsitien Lin. 1937.

The Sino-Japanese Conflict, by M. Hsitien Lin. 1937.

International Law and the Undeclared War, by Mousheng Hsitien Lin. 1937.

The Significance to the World of the Conflict in the Far East, by W. W. Willoughby. 1937.

Lightning Source UK Ltd.
Milton Keynes UK
UKHW051558170223
417096UK00041B/339

9 781258 675837